Grade Six Art Lessons: T

Learning Expectations with Art Activities

Knowledge of Elements	Corresponding Lesson
• Identify colour relationships, using a basic colour wheel	• Colour Wheel • Edible Colour Wheel • Complementary Colour Study • Colour Wheel 2 • Warm and Cool Colours
• Demonstrate understanding that shadows and shading create the illusion of a third dimension	• Shadow Butterflies • Shadow Dancing • Optical Illusions
• Describe how one-point perspective can be used to create the illusion of depth	• Picture Making Centre of Interest • Reflections in a Pond • Tom Thompson
▪ Identify things to be considered when placing a sculpture in a specific location	• Journal entries • Portfolio entries • Ongoing class discussion
• Identify the most appropriate tools, materials, and techniques for the size and scope of the work and use them correctly	• Journal entries • Portfolio entries • Ongoing class discussion
• Develop an awareness and appreciation of Canadian Artists	• Alex Janvier – bead designs • Daphne Odjig • Kananginak Pootoogook – Faux Antique Copper Foil Pictures • Cathay Edwards • David Ruben Piqtoukun – Inukshuks • Faye Heavyshields • Hoñgeeýesa • Fred Brown – Printing with Styrofoam Plates • Tom Thompson • Pitseolak Ashoona – Sand Sculptures • Maud Lewis

Creative Work	Corresponding Lesson
• Organize their art to create an effect, using the elements of design	• Alex Janvier – bead designs • Print Making – Blocks Prints • Print Making – Texture • Basic Stenciling • Print Making – Transfer Prints • Watercolour Techniques • Salt Prints • Maud Lewis
▪ Produce two and three-dimensional work	• Paper Mask Making • Paper Clay Planetscapes • Cool Kaleidoscope • Pitseolak Ashoona – Sand Sculptures
▪ Identify strengths and areas for improvement in their own work and that of others	• Journal entries • Portfolio entries • Ongoing class discussion
▪ Describe, in their plan for a work of art, how they will research their subject matter	• Journal entries • Portfolio entries • Ongoing class discussion

Learning Expectations with Art Activities

Critical thinking	Corresponding lesson
▪ Compare works from various periods and cultures, and describe how the artists have used the elements and principles of design	• Journal entries • Portfolio entries • Ongoing class discussion • Vincent Van Gogh – Starry Night • El Greco • Modern-day Pointillism
▪ Demonstrate awareness that an artist intentionally uses some of the elements and principles of design to convey meaning, and explain how the artist accomplishes his or her intentions	• Journal entries • Portfolio entries • Ongoing class discussion. • Vincent Van Gogh – Starry Night • El Greco • Alex Janvier – bead designs • Daphne Odjig • Kananginak Pootoogook – Faux Antique Copper Foil Pictures • Cathay Edwards • David Ruben Piqtoukun – Inukshuks • Faye Heavyshields • Hoñgeeýesa • Fred Brown – Printing with Styrofoam Plates • Tom Thompson • Pitseolak Ashoona – Sand Sculptures • Maud Lewis
▪ Identify the role art plays in multicultural traditions.	• Multicultural Crafts • Hoñgeeýesa • Masks

Art Concepts Covered

Line:

Lines are a provocation to exploration. Lines may be straight, curved, jagged, broken, solid, horizontal, vertical, diagonal, fat, thin, regular, and irregular, long or short! Children develop an awareness of lines and suggested movement by working through the outlined activities. Encourage children to develop this awareness through activities such as weaving, sculpting, painting, and finger painting.

Shape:

The activities in this book will expose children to natural, symbolic, geometric and representational or abstract shapes found in their environment. The lessons include doing drawings based on outlines, modeling, sculpting, building with boxes, tubes or paper mache, painting and pattern making.

Colour:

The colour activities will introduce the children to tone, intensity, value, and paint consistency. The concepts of primary, secondary, warm, and cool colour relationships may also be taught through these lessons.

Texture:

The surface quality, including appearance, tactile and visual effects may be explored through a number of the lessons in this book. Activities that involve the concept of texture include painting, weaving, sculpture, finger painting, paper mache, and fabric work.

Art Concepts Covered

Children learn art techniques through experimentation, demonstration, observation, and dialogue. Whenever possible, suggestions have been made to the teacher on how to include these concepts in the lessons.

Please remember that visual art techniques are not an end to themselves, but a means to develop the expression of ideas. It is necessary for children to have time to explore and use materials to practise the skills acquired.

Painting Skills:

Children should develop the following painting skills:

- how to put paint on the brush (paint should not spread onto the metal part of the brush);
- controlling paint (painting in large and small areas, varying the size of the lines);
- washing the brush before changing colours;
- mixing hues;
- painting next to dry and wet paint;
- painting over dry and wet paint;
- applying a wash;
- mixing tints and shades;
- blending colours;
- creating texture with paint;
- making smooth edges;
- combining paint and other media.

Pasting Skills

Apply bonding agents in a variety of ways, such as with brushes, applicators, fingers, toothpicks, scraps of paper, etc. Glue should not be visible on the finished product. Choosing a suitable adhesive as well as the placement and manipulation of the paste is a part of the skill development along with:

- applying small amounts of glue around the edges of the project;
- applying small amounts at strategic points on the project;
- applying glue to the shape not the background;
- applying pressure for a short time until the glue sticks.

Art Concepts Covered

Cutting or Tearing Skills:

Children should develop the following skills in the use of scissors:

- holding the scissors correctly;
- manipulating the paper and scissors;
- cutting a shape without the use of a pencil;
- cutting in even strokes;
- turning the paper to adapt to the scissors.

Tearing paper is different from ripping paper. When paper is ripped, it is an uncontrolled action. Tearing suggests control and the following techniques:

- using a short spreading movement to tear;
- or using the thumb and forefinger to tear.

Crayon and Stick Media:

Crayons, chalk, markers, oil pastels, and charcoal are only a few stick media, which can be:

- used heavily or lightly;
- blended, smeared, or dotted;
- polished, heated, ironed, or grooved;
- used under or over other media such as paint.

Modeling and Sculpting Materials

Various materials have been suggested for modeling and sculpting in this book. The teacher may also wish to change the medium to include some of the following suggestions:

- oil-based clay;
- water-based clay;
- starch & salt;
- paper mache;
- carving medium (mixing Plaster of Paris with sawdust, sand or vermiculite will make an excellent product for carving);
- card board box and tubes;
- sawdust and paste.

Vocabulary and Definitions

Abstract art: Is a style of art that attains its effect by altering visual elements rather than making things or people recognizable.

Advancing Colours: These colours seem to jump to the front of a painting. They are warm or vivid colours such as reds and yellows.

Black: The colour black is the absence of light. Paint pigment called black actually has other colours such as blue or brown added to it. Adding black to a colour may make it appear dull.

Blending: May be the mixing of two or more colours together, or creating a gradual change between colours.

Burnishing: Polishing or compressing the colour. Burnishing in coloured pencil drawings may be accomplished with a white pencil (or lighter colour of the colour being used) and rubbing over the area. This will iron out the grain of the paper compressing the pigment, creating a slight shine on the surface. Burnishing increases the brilliance of the colours. Rubbing a spoon or similar flat object over the paper to compress it may also burnish the surface.

Collage: Creating a picture by gluing pieces of materials such as paper, photos, magazine clippings, or found objects to a flat surface.

Colour: The eye sees colour when light bounces off an object. The "properties" of colour are hue, saturation, value and temperature.

Colour wheel: This tool organizes colours and represents relationships among them.

Complementary Colours: Complementary colours are colours that are opposite each other on the colour wheel. For example: yellow and violet.

Composition: Compositions are a balance of positive and negative spaces. Interesting compositions may be created by varying the shapes, textures and values.

Contrast: May be achieved by placing opposite colours beside one another. (rough/smooth, light/dark complementary colours)

Cool colours: Soothing colours such as greens, blues and violets are considered cool colours. They seem to retreat into the background or distance.

Crosshatching: drawing lines crossing each other in different directions may create volume or shading in a picture. The closer the lines, the darker the shading.

Vocabulary and Definitions

Dry brush: Pulling the paint out of the brush by dabbing the brush on a paper towel, or similar surface before painting. This will causes the brush to skip on the surface of the paper or canvas producing a broken effect. This is particularly good for creating the look of wood or texture.

Elements of design: These are the fundamental components of art works. They include colour, line, texture, shape, form, and space.

Focal point: The viewer's attention is focused upon the element or object in a work of art.

Form: Is an element of design. Form is sculptural or three-dimensional shape (e.g., cube, pyramid, sphere).

Frottage: From the French word "frotter," to rub. Texture is created when paper is placed over a textured surface and rubbed with a pencil, pastel, etc. causing the texture to be reproduced on the surface of the paper. This is often called a rubbing.

Highlights: Small light areas can add the finishing touch to a painting, and make it look professional. The sparkle on water, sunlight on the edges of a house or snow on a rooftop make the painting come to life!

Hue: Is the common name of a colour (e.g., blue).

Impressionistic art. A characteristic of the Impressionist style is the depiction of the effect of light on objects.

Monochromatic: A painting done in different shades and tints of one colour.

Perspective: Is a technique for creating the illusion of depth on a two-dimensional surface. There are three types of perspective:

- **linear perspective:** This involves the use of parallel lines that appear to converge in the distance; (Think railroad tracks!)
- **diminishing perspective:** Objects appear to diminish in size as their distance from the viewer increases; (Think telephone poles!)
- **atmospheric perspective:** This is produced by the gradual lessening of the intensity of colour and the reducing of detail as the distance between an object and the viewer increases. (Think foggy night!)

Pointillism: A style of painting commonly attributed to Georges Seurat; it is created when small dots of colour are placed close together. From a distance, the dots disappear and the colours blend to form the image.

Vocabulary and Definitions

Principles of design: Guidelines used by artists to organize the visual elements of an artwork. These include balance, emphasis, rhythm, unity, movement, variety, harmony, and proportion.

Primary Colours: These are the basic colours, red, blue and yellow, from which all other colours can be mixed. Mixtures of these produce the secondary colours, orange, green and violet.

Secondary Colours: These are colours produced from the mixture of even amounts of two primary colours. Blue and red makes violet, yellow and red makes orange, and blue and yellow makes green.

Sgraffito: A technique created by scratching into paint to reveal the colours underneath.

Shade. A colour with black added.

Tertiary Colours: Mixing unequal amounts of two primary colours produces these colours. For example, adding more red to the combination of red and yellow will produce the tertiary color of red-orange. Tertiary colours are located between the primary and secondary colours on a colour wheel.

Tint. A colour with white added.

Value: Value is the lightness or darkness of a colour.

Wash: Is created by adding water to paint, making it thin enough to allow colours applied underneath to show through.

Warm Colours: The colours in the yellow to red range are considered warm colours. They make us think of such things as the sun and fire. Warm colours are used to make an object appear to advance into the foreground.

About Picture Making Skills

Picture making is an excellent form of art expression. Give children regular opportunities to develop their abilities. Motivation for picture making may come from several sources at once, including children's sensory perceptions, feelings, experiences, ideas, tools, materials, and theme suggestions from the teacher.

Interesting materials with which to paint:

- Fingers
- Branches
- Rags
- Brushes
- Plastic pot scrubbers
- Sticks
- Rope
- Sponges
- Cotton swabs
- Cork
- Blocks of wood
- Feathers
- Toothpicks
- Cotton balls
- Foam

Interesting tools with which to draw:

- Crayons
- Chalk
- Felt tip markers
- Pencils
- Charcoal
- Make up
- Fingers
- Ink pens
- Pencil crayons

Interesting surfaces on which to paint or draw:

- Newsprint
- Tissue paper
- Glass (windows)
- Plastic wrap
- Aluminum foil
- Paper plates
- Paper bags
- Cardboard
- Paper towels
- Stones
- Blocks of wood
- Crepe paper
- Cloth
- Waxed paper
- Foam

Suggestions on how to organize a picture-making centre:

- Permit time for the activity;
- Some activities may need more than one class depending on the students and the schedule;
- Have children work in groups. Four is a practical number;
- Assign "job numbers" to each member of the group;
- Keep work where children will be able to allow it to dry, and reclaim it easily (Clothes lines of string with pegs make it easy for young children to hang their paintings to dry).

How To Organize Your Classroom For Art Instruction

Physical Set Up:

Organize the classroom to allow for storage and work areas.

- Position storage areas so that children can find and return supplies;
- Water tins are a part of cleanup in a paint area, so a rational place for the paint area would be close to a sink. If a sink is not available, an area of the floor or table may be covered with newspaper or plastic drop sheets and a bucket of water may be used for cleaning;
- Turn up rinsed water tins on a pad of newspaper and allow to dry to prevent rusting;
- Store brushes with the bristles up to prevent distortion, by placing them in a tall empty juice can;
- If cupboards are not available to store paints, consider a large plastic milk bin or cardboard box.

How To Organize Your Classroom For Art Instruction

Supplies and Materials:

Encourage children to experiment with a variety of media, materials, and tools. Teach lessons on how to care for and maintain the equipment, as well as organize it. The following is a list of suggested materials needed for a good visual arts program:

- **crayons:** Try to provide a variety of sizes, as well as other stick materials such as oil pastels, markers, coloured pencils, and charcoal;
- **paper:** A variety of papers about 45 cm. X 60 cm. should be used. Manila and newsprint are some types of paper recommended. Other papers such as craft paper, finger painting paper, construction paper or corrugated paper may be suggested in the materials lists;
- **scissors**: A good set of scissors is necessary for facility of cutting. Points of the scissors should be rounded, and a few left handed pairs should be available;
- **paint:** Water-based tempera is used most often. Mixing a small amount of dish detergent into the paint will make it easier to wash out of clothing;
- **brushes:** Generally a 1.5 cm. brush is used for projects, but students should have access to a variety of sizes and shapes to apply paint in lines, large masses, patterns or textures;
- **other media:** Be innovative in allowing children to experiment with natural and found materials such as twigs, leaves, stones, cloth, cardboard, foam, and commercial materials such as wool, wire, toothpicks, plastiscene, finger-paint, burlap, etc.

How To Organize Your Classroom For Art Instruction

Before Beginning a Visual Arts Lesson:

- Assemble the materials and supplies necessary for the lesson;
- Have the children arrange their desks, or tables in groups of four (it may be necessary to allow some children to work on the floor);
- When the time comes, have the children distribute supplies according to their "job numbers".

Routines:

The emphasis should be on an orderly and well-organized distribution and set-up. The participation of students in as many of the responsibilities as possible is optimal. The children should understand the expectations and be involved in the routines of clean-up and organization.

Distribution of Materials:

Assign each child or member of a group a "job number" so that they may have a specific chore to do during set up and clean up time. For example:

- <u>number one</u> will get the newspaper and put it away;
- <u>number two</u> will get the water and pour it out after art time;
- <u>number three</u> will get the brushes and clean the brushes;
- <u>number four</u> will get the drawing paper and collect finished work.

Clean-up:

- Usually ten minutes is enough time to allow for clean-up, depending on the age and motivation of the group;
- Place an emphasis on orderliness and the development of useful work habits;
- Children should assume total responsibility for clean up.

Art Centres

In order to run successful visual arts centres, good planning on the part of the teacher is essential. Follow these steps:

FIRST: Examine your timetable and decide on one time block to devote consistently as art centres time.

SECOND: Decide how many centres will be set up during art centres and what they will be.

THIRD: Store what is needed for each activity in an individual bin. In this way, centres are organized and ready to go. Each centre bin should include:

- All materials needed to complete the activity for each child;
- A sample of completed work to show students.

FOURTH: Introduce and explain the expectation of each learning centre to the class. This is the time to teach any specific skills, needed to complete a centre. In addition, review how many students are allowed at each centre.

If a learning centre approach is new to your classroom, balance your centres so that some of the activities will need minimum teacher direction, such as a free exploration painting centre. This will allow students an opportunity to learn how to work independently and with other students.

Check Points for Teachers:

- ☑ Encourage children to do their own work;
- ☑ Exhibit all of the children's work;
- ☑ Encourage children to be inventive;
- ☑ Encourage children to finish their work;
- ☑ Encourage children to talk about their work using art vocabulary;
- ☑ Provide ample time and opportunity for art;
- ☑ Teach children to care for materials;
- ☑ Encourage children to experiment with various media;
- ☑ Encourage children to be observant and aware of their environment;
- ☑ Be enthusiastic and have fun! There is no right or wrong!

A Word About Materials

The materials used in this book are typically the type found in most elementary schools. On occasion it is suggested that some materials be purchased in craft supply stores, but whenever possible standard school supplies have been suggested.

Paint:

Tempera paint can be in powder, block (or pan) or liquid form. The powdered tempera should be mixed with water before using. Solid blocks of paint (called pans) can be placed in muffin tins to contain the paint nicely.
Gouache is thick and opaque. It can be used without mixing with water and nice bright colours can be obtained.
Acrylic paint can be bought in tubes or bottles. They are often used in folk or decorative art. Sometimes these can be purchased for minimal cost at craft supply store. They can be thinned with water and are easy cleaned if done immediately. Don't let it dry!

Pastels & crayons:

Oil pastels have a brighter effect than chalk pastels. Both blend nicely, but oil pastels tend to be a little less messy!
Wax crayons may be substituted for oil pastels if the activity does not call for the work to be blended. Crayons are excellent for resists and etching into the waxy surface.

Inks:

Coloured inks come in bottles, but an alternative to buying large quantities is to use ink cartridges. Just split them apart and squeeze out the ink!

Markers:

Markers are wonderful tools for children to use. Permanent markers can be used to add details to paintings, drawings and whenever accents that do not bleed are needed. They will mark over most surfaces including acrylic paint. Markers that are not permanent can result in lovely effects when used over a wet surface. To create alternative effects, you may draw over them with a wet medium. For example, run a bead of glue over a water marker surface for "puffy" effects.

What kind of paper?

There are several different types of paper, from the common computer print-out paper, to lovely Japanese rice papers. How can you decide what paper is the right type for the project on which you are embarking? Here are few definitions that may help:

Cartridge Paper:

- use with inks or pastels
- heavier than photocopy paper
- slightly rougher surface to "grab" medium
- can withstand being wet

Tissue Paper:

- thin
- polished surface
- transparent
- bleeds when wet
- fragile

Watercolour Paper:

- specially formulated to withstand being wet
- needs to be taped down to prevent warping
- comes in different weights (40 lbs. will suit most purposes)
- cold press has rougher surface
- hot press allows watercolour to float on surface for longer periods

Newsprint:

- thin
- use for projects that do not require permanence
- absorbs ink and water easily
- is newspaper before the printing
- good for the last layer of a paper mache project

Rice paper:

- usually expensive
- used in projects that require strength
- usually can be recognized by a fibre-like thread through paper

Did you know?

- Make sand clay by combining 250 ml. of cornstarch, 500ml. of sifted sand and 325ml. of water. Cook in an old pot for 10 minutes, or until mixture leaves the side of the pot. Cool, knead and store in an airtight container.

- Mixing 1 part white glue and 1 part tempera paint will give the paint a shiny wet look.

- To make bookbinding glue you combine 1 package of unflavoured gelatin, 3 tablespoons of boiling water, 1 tablespoon of vinegar and 1 teaspoon of glycerin. Add gelatin to water. Stir until dissolved. Add vinegar and glycerin. Stir until well mixed. Binds leather-to-leather or cloth to cardboard for notebook binders or scrapbooks. Makes about 1/3 cup.

- 2 teaspoons of salt mixed with 1 teaspoon of liquid starch makes icy pictures.

- Egg yolks, dry detergent and food colouring together makes a paint that will stick to any surface.

- Mixing equal parts of liquid starch and cold water makes an excellent paper mache glue.

- You can make bakers clay by mixing 2 cups of flour, 1 cup of salt and water, and baking at 300 degrees.

- To make no bake dough that stays soft, use the above recipe, but add 2 tablespoons of oil.

- Corn syrup painted over a surface gives a shiny, leathery, golden finish. (May take a long time to dry on humid days!)

- To make tempera paint brighter and easier to wash out, add liquid starch and liquid soap in a 2:1 ratio.

- To dye pasta quickly and make bright colours, you should pour a small amount of rubbing alcohol into the food colouring before dropping in the uncooked pasta.

- You can make "ink" for printing with heavy-duty vinyl adhesive from Colour Your World. Colour with the paint tints used to colour paint, and add "retarder" to keep the mix from drying out too soon. This makes a cheap substitute for more expensive printing ink, and works very well!

September Art Lessons

Try these art centres:

- ❖ Put tempera paint in a spray bottle. Spray a misty area around the edges of a leaf.
- ❖ Trace classroom objects, such as scissors, rulers, etc on magazine pages. Outline objects in black marker and make a collage.
- ❖ Colour shades of one coloured pencil progressing from light to dark down the paper.
- ❖ Listen to music while "doodling" shapes to the rhythm. Do not lift your pencil. Colour the doodles.
- ❖ Tear tissue paper into leaf shapes and dampen. Place along a painted branch. When dry, remove the tissue paper leaving a print behind.
- ❖ Make a garland of leaves, fruit or vegetables to drape around the room.

Alex Janvier

The First Nations People of Canada have been creating art for many, many years. When non-native people came to North America, they collected and traded tools made by native people. The non-native people did not always understand the beauty of the Native Art, but artists like Alex Janvier helped to make Native Art an important part of Canada.

Alex Janvier was born in 1935. He was raised on the Le Goffe Reserve in Cold Lake Alberta. He studied at the Alberta College of Art and graduated in 1960. Alex Janvier paints pictures that seem to flow across the canvas. He likes to draw traditional native beadwork designs and many of the things that have happened to the First Nations people in Canada. You can see examples of his art at www.mcmichael.com

Many beautiful designs are found in Native beadwork. Use the following activity to create designs that emulate this beadwork.

Beadwork Designs

Time Frame: 40 minutes

MATERIALS:

- Square graph paper
- Assorted markers
- Examples of native beadwork or pictures

WHAT TO DO:

1. After viewing examples of native beadwork, distribute graph paper to each of the children. The graph paper should be 10 squares x 50 squares;
2. Model for the children how to create a design on their graph paper, like a bird, tree or any traditional native picture;
3. Next have children colour their design using colours of their choice;
4. The teacher may wish to read with the class several native stories and legends to act as inspiration for the children.

Cool Socks

Time Frame: 40 minutes plus drying time

MOTIVATION:

Be cool. Create a classroom of togetherness! Have your students create a pair of socks to be worn by each student in your class!

WHAT YOU NEED:

- Fabric dyes in different colours (since this is permanent, use disposable materials)
- Pans or tubs of warm water
- Rubber gloves
- Elastic bands
- Plastic spoons
- Pre-washed white cotton socks that are wet
- Newspaper

WHAT TO DO:

1. Dissolve the dyes in the tubs making dye baths of different colours;
2. Demonstrate for the students how to wrap elastic bands tightly around the white socks; (To make a matching pair, wrap both the socks together)
3. Taking care not to drop any dye on your clothing, show the children how to dip socks one section at a time into the dye baths;
4. Rinse the socks in cold water, and lay on newspaper to dry;
5. Once dry, remove the rubber bands, and enjoy your cool socks!

TEACHER TIP:

Washing tip: Wash separately in case the dye runs the first few times!

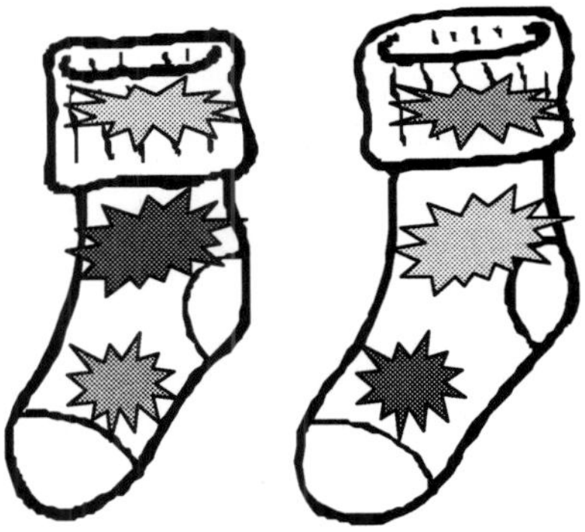

Colour Wheel

Time Frame: 40 minutes

MOTIVATION:

The primary colours are red, blue, and yellow. They are called primary colours because they cannot be created by mixing. Mixing these colours together creates all other colours. The teacher may wish to stop at the creation of the secondary colours, or continue to mix the secondary colours to create the tertiary colours.

WHAT YOU NEED:

- Red, blue and yellow tempera paint
- Paint brushes
- Drawing paper
- Template of a large triangle and a circle which is sized to touch each tip of the triangle
- Template of small circles

WHAT TO DO:

1. Using the template, draw a large triangle;
2. Place the large circle over the triangle, so that the triangle is centered on the circle;
3. At the tip of each vertices of the triangle, trace the smaller circle;
4. Paint the top circle red, the circle on the bottom left blue and the remaining circle yellow;
5. These are the primary colours;
6. Between each of these three circles, trace another small circle;
7. Paint the circle between the blue and red circle purple, by mixing the red and blue paint;
8. Paint the circle between the blue and yellow circle green, by mixing the yellow and blue paint;
9. Paint the circle between the red and yellow circle orange, by mixing the red and yellow;
10. These are the secondary colours;

TEACHER TIP:

To easily demonstrate how mixing the colours create new colours, create the above activity using food colouring on an overhead projector. When the colours have been dropped on the projector, place a plastic acetate sheet over the drops to blend and amaze!

Edible Colour Wheel

Time Frame: 40 minutes

Motivation:

Once children have discovered the primary colours red, blue, and yellow, they can have fun mixing and eating their frosted colour wheel.

What you need:

- Red, blue and yellow gelatin powder (e.g strawberry, blueberry, lemon)
- White canned frosting (2-3 cans per class)
- Plastic knives or Popsicle sticks
- Wax paper
- Plastic spoons
- Plain round cookies (sugar or vanilla type)

What to do:

1. Place 3 dollops of white frosting on the wax paper;
2. Demonstrate for the children how to use the plastic spoon to scoop a small amount of gelatin powder into the frosting;
3. Mix using the plastic knife or Popsicle stick;
4. Keep adding gelatin powder until a vibrant colour of red, blue and yellow is obtained in each dollop;
5. Using the plastic knife or Popsicle stick, spread a small amount of frosting on a cookie;
6. Place these cookie at the primary colour points on the colour wheel; (blackline master of wheel on next page)
7. Demonstrate for the children how to use a small portion of the remaining coloured frosting to create the secondary colours of orange, green and purple;
8. Using the plastic knife or Popsicle stick, frost the cookies with the secondary colours;
9. Place the secondary colour cookies next to the primary colour cookies to replicate the colour wheel;
10. Continue mixing the colours to obtain the tertiary colours (see definitions) and frost another set of cookie;
11. Place these cookies in the appropriate place on the wheel;
12. Discuss the process of making the colour wheel with the students;
13. Eat!

Complementary Colour Study

Blackline master

Use this sheet to create the colour palette an artist would use to learn about the colours and how they mix. Complementary colours are opposite each other on the colour wheel.

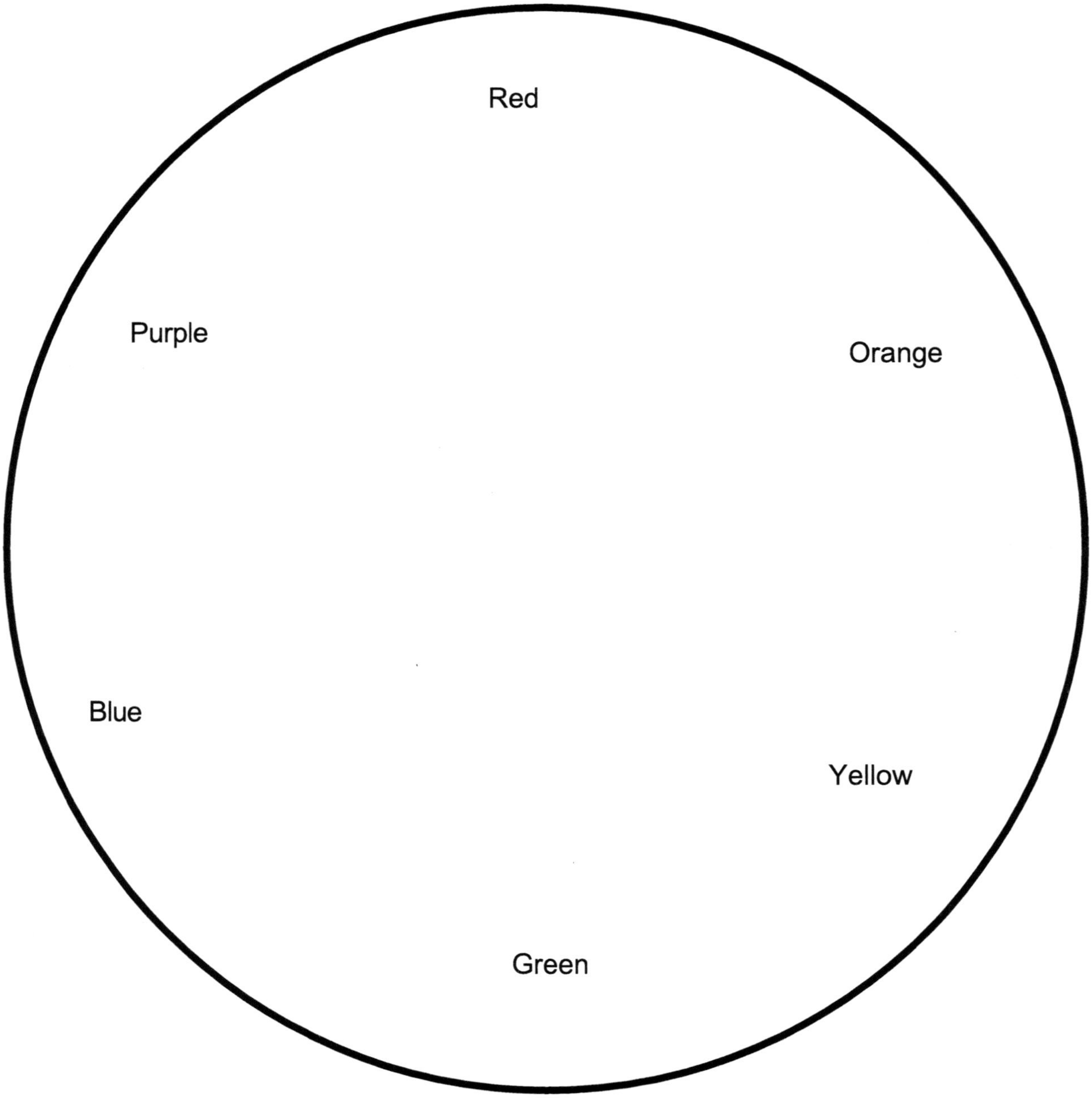

Bobble Head Self Portraits

Time Frame: 40 minutes after developing pictures

MOTIVATION:

Create big headed “bobble” students. The students may like to write words that best express their personality around the “bobble head”.

Digital cameras are becoming part of everyone’s lifestyle. If possible, a digital camera should be used in this project.

WHAT YOU NEED:

- Digital camera
- Scissors
- Glue
- Colouring materials
- Manila paper

WHAT YOU DO:

1. Using the camera, take two pictures of each student;
2. The first picture should be a close-up of their head;
3. The second picture should be a far away shot of their body;
4. Have the pictures printed on photocopy paper;
5. Demonstrate for the students how to carefully cut out their head and body pictures;
6. Show them how to glue down the body and head to form a “Bobble head doll”;
7. Using the markers colour over the details of the picture, accentuating the big head and small body;
8. Create a background for your bobble head doll adding details.

October Lessons

Try these art centres:

- ❖ Make an observational drawing of a cornucopia.
- ❖ Add food colouring to white glue. Draw on a juice tin lid using the coloured glue. When dry, peel off and use as sun catcher.
- ❖ Make a night scene by gluing black silhouettes on grey paper. Highlight the reflection of the moon on the black silhouettes with white chalk.
- ❖ Colour a picture using oil pastels and only shades of orange and black.
- ❖ Twist green tissue paper into "vines" and glue on "pumpkins". Variation: black tissue with ghosts and skeletons
- ❖ Tie elastics around coffee filters and dip into concentrated Koolaid. Cut off elastics for tie-dyed effect.

Halloween Activities

Crayon resist:

Draw a Halloween scene using crayons. Colouring objects heavily with crayon creates the best results. Wash or paint over the crayon with watered down paint. The paint is at the correct consistency when the crayon resists the paint and the crayon shows through.

Pastels on coloured construction paper:

Bright pastels look most effective on black construction paper. Be sure the students are aware of fingerprints showing on the pictures, and that they are careful not to smear the pastels. "Fix" the pictures (fixing them makes the pastels no longer subject to smearing) by applying a spray of cheap hairspray. The less expensive, the better!

Other ideas:

Black crayon, coloured chalk or tempera paint on orange, grey or yellow construction paper.

White paint or white oil pastel on black construction paper.

Tempera paint in orange, black and yellow on the daily newspaper makes interesting, spooky effects.

White crayon and a dark tempera paint wash on manila paper.

Body paint:

Lard mixed with food coloring. Heat the lard in the microwave, pour into an empty film container and mix with the food coloring of your choice!

Bloody Fingers

Time Frame: two periods - one of 20 minutes and one of 40 minutes

MOTIVATION:

What better way to get into the fun of Halloween than to place a "bloody finger" in door jams, on window sills, or in a bowl of chips!

WHAT YOU NEED:

- Disposable rubber gloves
- Plaster of Paris
- Acrylic or tempera paints in skin tones and red
- Elastics

WHAT TO DO:

In the first lesson:

1. Demonstrate for the students how to mix the Plaster of Paris;
2. Carefully pour the Plaster of Paris into one of the fingers of the glove;
3. Show how to wrap an elastic around the finger to prevent the Plaster of Paris from leaking out;
4. Allow the Plaster of Paris to dry;

In the next lesson:

1. Show the student how to tear away the rubber glove from the Plaster of Paris fingers;
2. Using the tempera or acrylic paint, decorate the fingers with bloody stumps and "nail polish", rings or other details!

TEACHER TIP:

To measure the amount of plaster of Paris needed, fill the fingers in the glove with water and pour into a measuring cup. This is the amount of plaster mix you will require, per set of fingers!

Golf Ball and Marble Art

Time Frame: 40 minutes

MOTIVATION:

Create unique line drawings using golf balls and marbles! Add some spiders, bats or skeletons to create a Halloween scene.

WHAT YOU NEED:

- Two or three marbles
- One golf ball
- Tempera paint
- Tubs to contain the paint
- Pans (cookie, tinfoil, casserole, etc.)
- Drawing paper cut to fit the pans
- Spoons
- Water
- Paper towel

WHAT TO DO:

1. Fill tubs with tempera paint;
2. Place a piece of paper inside the pan;
3. Carefully drop the marbles, and golf ball into the tubs of paint;
4. Scoop out marbles and golf ball one at a time;
5. Roll marble or golf ball over the paper in the pan by tipping and turning the pan;
6. Remove marble or golf ball and repeat until all colours have been applied to the paper;
7. Wash & dry marbles and golf ball;
8. Remove paper from pan and allow to dry;
9. Voila! A line drawing of amazing interest!

Warm and Cool Colours

Time Frame: 40 minutes

Cool colours are considered to be on the right side of the colour wheel, including green, blue and purple.
Warm colours are considered to be on the left side of the colour wheel, including red, yellow and orange.

MOTIVATION:

Artists such as Vincent van Gogh used colour to create a mood or express emotion in a picture by using only warm or cool colours. We call this a monochromatic painting. Students may wish to add a contrasting accent.

WHAT YOU NEED:

- Manila paper
- Colouring materials
- Pencil

WHAT TO DO:

1. Demonstrate for the children how to fold the paper into eight sections;
2. Have the students brainstorm different moods or emotions.
3. Write them lightly on the back of each section of the paper;
4. Draw each mood on the other side, using colors, shapes and lines to best show the mood;
5. Share the drawings with a friend;
6. Ask if they can guess what mood or emotion you drew.

Daphne Odjig

Daphne Odjig is a Canadian Woodland Native artist. She was born on the Wikwemikong Indian Reserve on Manitoulin Island and is a member of the Ojibwa tribe. She currently lives with her husband, Chester Beavon on Shuswap Lake just outside of Kamloops. Odjig's style is based on the abstracted human form. The Ojibwa symbol for woman is the circle. Odjig uses the circle as a central design in her work. Her mural for the foyer of the National Art Centre in Ottawa is called *The Indian in Transition* and is 27 feet!
Learn more about Daphne Odjig at: http://www.kstrom.net/isk/art/odjig/art_odj.html

---

Time Frame: 40 minutes

MOTIVATION:

Many of Daphne Odjig's paintings have a circular or round theme. In this activity the students will draw inside a circle. Drawing in a circle eliminates a flat bottom for the ground, or edge for the sky. Some pictures lend themselves well to be in a circle. You may wish to brainstorm with your students some ideas before beginning.

WHAT YOU NEED:

- Large sheets of manila or drawing paper
- Scissors
- Colouring or painting materials
- Large circular object such as a pizza pan or a large compass

WHAT TO DO:

1. Demonstrate for the children how to trace around the pizza pan or other round object to make a circular shape on the large drawing paper;
2. Cut out the circle;
3. Draw a picture on the round shape;
4. Colour or paint.

TEACHER TIP: Some "round" ideas:
Fish bowl, portholes, tires, coins, planets, moons, puddles, etc.

Colour Wheel 2

Time Frame: 40 minutes

MOTIVATION:

PRIMARY COLORS: red, yellow and blue
These are the 3 pigment colors that can not be mixed or formed by any combination of other colors. All other colors are derived from these 3 hues
SECONDARY COLORS: green, orange and purple
These are the colors formed by mixing the primary colors.
TERTIARY COLORS: yellow-orange, red-orange, red-purple, blue-purple, blue-green and yellow-green.
These are the colors formed by mixing the secondary colors.

WHAT YOU NEED:

- Bristol board
- 3 pieces of Cellophane paper -- red, blue, and yellow (rolls of cellophane paper can be bought at most craft stores, where wrapping paper is sold)
- White glue
- Scissors
- Hole punch
- Paper fastener (brad tack)

WHAT TO DO:

1. Demonstrate for the students how to draw a rectangle;
2. Cut out the centre of the rectangle to create a "window", leaving a border of about two centimetres;
3. Trace this rectangle six times onto Bristol board;
4. Cut the cellophane smaller than the outside of the frame, but larger than the inside;
5. Sandwich a coloured piece of cellophane between two pieces of cut out Bristol board;
6. Glue the two pieces of Bristol board together to make a window;
7. Repeat until all three windows are made;
8. Once all three "windows" are dry stack on top of each other and punch a hole in the center of the bottom end and fasten together with a paper fastener;
9. As the fan is opened and closed over the coloured cellophane, the primary, secondary and tertiary colours are displayed.

November Art Lessons

Try these art centres:

- ❖ Make an observational drawing of a running shoe.
- ❖ Drop blobs of thin paint on paper. Using drinking straws, blow shapes on the paper. Turn the shapes into faces, trees etc.
- ❖ Place a piece of paper in the bottom of a shoebox. Drop blobs of paint onto the paint and roll a marble through the paint making tracks on the white paper.
- ❖ Roll out a large piece of paper and have 5 children on a signal, rotate around the paper, painting as they go!
- ❖ Tack long strips of black construction paper over murals to make it appear as if you are looking through a window.
- ❖ Practise colouring a colouring page on different surfaces, such as sandpaper to create texture.

Poppy Wreaths

Time Frame: 40 minutes

MOTIVATION:
Every year on November 11, at eleven o'clock in the morning, Canadians stop and pay tribute to the many Canadian soldiers who sacrificed their lives for our country. The following activity is an excellent way to acquaint children with the sacrifices made by Canadian soldiers, by creating a tissue paper wreath of poppies.

MATERIALS:

- Red and black tissue paper
- Scissors
- Stapler or pipe cleaners
- Bristol Board wreath (red is preferred but not necessary)

WHAT TO DO:

1. Have children lay 3 red layers of tissue paper flat on top of one another;
2. Lay one black piece of tissue paper on top of the red pile;
3. Model for the children how to fold the tissue paper back and forth as you would when making a paper fan;
4. Have children find the middle of the long strip;
5. Demonstrate for the children how to staple the tissue strip securely;
6. Model for the children how to round the ends of the tissue paper with scissors;
7. With the black piece in the centre, instruct the children to carefully pull apart the "petals" of the flowers, until all sheets are separated;
8. Attach all the flowers in a large wreath by gluing on the Bristol board circle.

TEACHER TIP:
Have the children use a blackboard compass to make the wreath on Bristol board.
Use this very attractive wreath in a Remembrance Day ceremony.

Popsicle Stick Puzzle

Time Frame: 40 minutes

MOTIVATION:

This activity can be used to create puzzles for your students to swap and solve. It is an easy and fun way for your students to express their feelings about a subject.

WHAT YOU NEED:

- Popsicle sticks
- Masking tape
- Markers or paint

WHAT TO DO:

1. Tape the Popsicle sticks together on the back, forming a square;
2. Create a picture on the front using the markers or paint;
3. Allow the sticks to dry before pulling off the tape;
4. Challenge a buddy to put your puzzle back together.

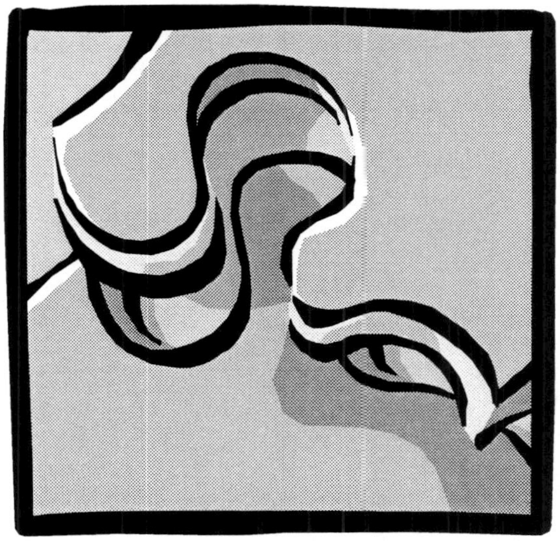

Print Making
Texture 1

Time Frame: 40 minutes

MOTIVATION:
Rubbing crayons or pastels over paper shapes creates single texture designs in this beginning lesson on texture and printmaking.

WHAT YOU NEED:
- Large sheets of newsprint
- Crayons or pastels
- Scissors
- Scrap pieces of construction paper
- Watered down tempera paint to make a wash (Optional)

WHAT TO DO:
1. Fold the newsprint in half;
2. Cut interesting shapes from the scrap construction paper;
3. Place the shapes on the inside half of the folded newsprint;
4. Fold the newsprint over the shapes;
5. Using the side of the crayon or pastel, rub the paper from edge to edge.

TEACHER TIP: Optional: After rubbing, wash the entire surface with a coat of watered down paint.

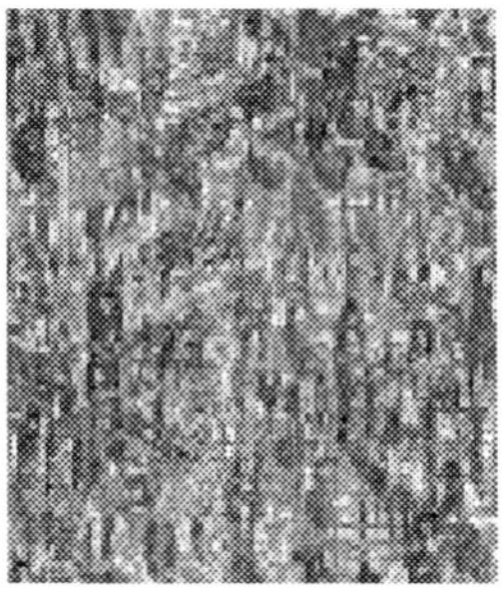

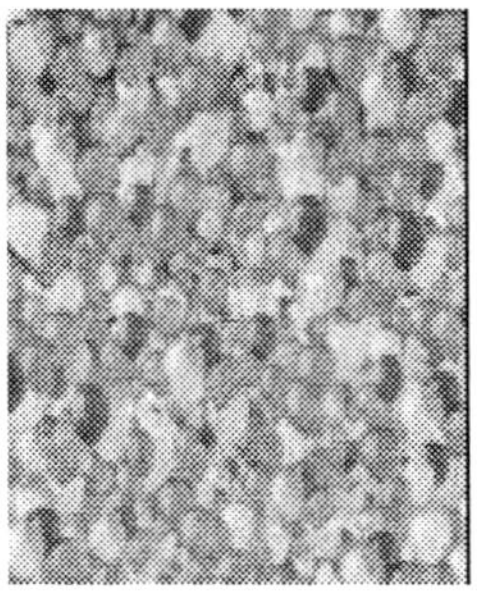

Paper Making Without a Blender!

Time Frame: 40 minutes

MOTIVATION:

Making paper is a wonderful way to stimulate writing and creating cards. In this activity, a minimal amount of equipment is necessary.

WHAT YOU NEED:

- Large tub or pan
- Large jar with tight lid
- Plastic spoon
- Hot water
- Rolling pin
- Mixing bowls
- Coloured paper
- Cornstarch
- Wax paper
- Measuring spoons & cups

WHAT TO DO:

1. Tear the paper into strips and then again into tiny pieces;
2. Fill the large jar with the tiny pieces of paper; (pickle jars are a good choice)
3. Fill the jar with hot water with the lid on and let stand for 3-4 hours;
4. When the jar is cool enough to touch, shake it vigorously, mixing the pieces of paper;
5. Continue to shake and stir the mixture with the plastic spoon, until the paper has broken down;
6. When the water is absorbed, add more hot water, until the mixture appears creamy and smooth;
7. Pour the mixture into the tub or pan;
8. Dissolve about 3 tablespoons of cornstarch in ½ cup of water and add to the tub of paper mix;
9. Place a piece of wax paper on a table;
10. Scoop out a handful of mixture and squeeze out the excess water;
11. Put this handful of mixture on the wax paper, and smooth out, adding more if necessary, in order to have a thin layer on top of the wax paper;
12. Place a second piece of wax paper over the top and press out with a rolling pin, mopping up the water that bleeds out;
13. Allow to dry before creating a card or note book cover.

Kananginak Pootoogook

Kananginak Pootoogook was born in 1953 in Cape Dorset. Pootoogook was one of the first artists in Cape Dorset to participate in printmaking. For many years he continued to work on his printmaking skills and produced beautiful work in stone, copper engraving and silk-screens. Pootoogook became known all over the world for keeping the Inuit traditions alive in his art.

Kananginak says he likes to think through his ideas in his mind, until he sees exactly what the painting, or sculpture looks like. Only when he is happy with the picture in his mind, does he start the real thing!

Copper engraving is when an artist uses tools to scratch or engrave a picture into the metal. The results are beautiful. Have your students create a "metal" drawing by trying this foil painting technique.

Faux Antique Copper Foil Pictures

Time Frame: 40 minutes

MOTIVATION:

Copper tooling is an art form that is created by "carving" into the soft copper metal sheets. The copper ages producing a verdigris patina over the surface. In this activity, the aging process is created with shoe polish, while the copper effect is raised instead of carved. This technique can be used for many projects, from making shields as props for plays, or medallions to wear, photo frames as gifts, or decorative "tiles" for borders.

WHAT YOU NEED:

- cardboard in the size appropriate for finished item (a medallion would use a small round piece, while a photo frame would be larger!)
- pencil
- white PVA glue
- black or brown shoe polish
- gold acrylic paint or aluminum foil
- soft cloth or cotton balls

WHAT TO DO:

1. Demonstrate for the students how to draw a simple design on the piece of cardboard;
2. Show the students how to trace over the design with the PVA glue;
3. Allow to dry;
4. Cover the design with gold acrylic paint or aluminum foil (if using aluminum foil, rub the surface gently, pressing the foil over the dried outlines) (if using the paint, allow to dry);
5. Using a soft cloth or cotton balls, apply the shoe polish and buff the surface until raised surfaces are outlined by the shoe polish.

December Art Lessons

Try these art centres:

❖ Candy cane reindeer are always a treat! At the end of the curled end of a candy cane, glue a red pompom. Glue on brown felt ears. Make antlers from pipe cleaners, and glue on googly eyes.

❖ Place a cedar branch flat on coloured paper. Spray with silver or gold spray. Use the branch to decorate and the paper for wrapping gifts!

❖ Cut 2 circles of wallpaper or old Christmas cards. Carefully cut the circles to the centre. Slip the slits together make an ornament.

❖ Scrape old crayons onto on wax paper. Place a second piece of wax paper over top. Press with a hot iron melting the crayon. Instant stained glass!

❖ Make a sparkling snowflake from aluminum foil, tinsel, and glitter.

❖ Glue two candy canes on the bottom of a square of chocolate to create a sleigh.

Multicultural Holiday Crafts

Hanukkah Stars

Create a Star of David.
Make shiny decorations from disposable aluminium pie plates or roasting pans. Use a nail to make indentations or to decorate the cut-out.

Kwanzaa

Kwanzaa gifts, called zawadi (zah-wah-dee), are made by hand. Make a Kwanzaa necklace using sand beads. Mix 250 ml. of sand with 60 ml. of white glue in a plastic or paper cup. Pinch off sand dough and roll a bead in the size you want. With a nail, poke a hole through the center for stringing. Let the bead dry on the tray until hard. String the beads to make a necklace. Beads may be decorated with markers or rolled in glue and sparkles for added glitz!

Ramadan Silhouettes

On wet Manila paper, have children create a dawn or dusk effect by applying streaks of yellow, orange and pink paint on the whole paper. Let the paper dry. Meanwhile have children cut out silhouettes of mosques and other buildings found in the community. Paste these silhouettes on the dry dusk or dawn paintings.

Holiday Spoon Gift

Melt chocolate in the microwave. Dip a plastic spoon in hot melted chocolate. Let it dry on wax paper. Next, decorate the spoon by wrapping a colourful ribbon around the handle and give to your favourite coffee drinker for a special stir!

Clay Tiles

Time Frame: two periods of 40 minutes

MOTIVATION:
If you are lucky enough to have a kiln available for use, terra cotta clay fired in a kiln makes a beautiful finished product. Self-drying clay can be very attractive and does not have to be kiln fired.

WHAT YOU NEED:

- Clay – self-hardening or kiln fired
- Variety of leaves or natural artifacts
- Rolling pin
- Wax paper
- Brown shoe polish – paste format
- Straw
- Plastic knife (optional)
- Ruler (optional)

WHAT TO DO:
1. Demonstrate for the students how to roll the clay out to a uniform thickness using the rolling pin;
2. If a clean edge is desired, cut the clay using a plastic knife and ruler; (optional)
3. Using a straw, pierce a hole at the top of the clay in order to create a means by which to hang the finished piece;
4. Place a leaf or other natural artifact on top of the clay;
5. Over the clay and leaf arrangement, lay a piece of wax paper;
6. Roll over the wax paper with the rolling pin, making an impression of the leaf or artifact in the clay;
7. Allow the clay to dry completely;
8. Remove the leaf or artifact;
9. If using kiln-fired clay, fire after a week of drying;
10. When clay is dry or fired, apply a thin coat of brown shoe polish.
11. Rub the paste into the fine lines and cracks of the clay to create a lovely patina.

TEACHER TIP: Makes a lovely gift!

Print Making

Block Prints

Time Frame: 40 minutes

MOTIVATION:

Simple print blocks can be made using a variety of materials. Display these prints on a bulletin board or use to make decorative wrapping paper.

WHAT YOU NEED:

- Thick cardboard squares
- Materials to create prints, such as rope, string, sponges, macaroni, etc.
- Glue
- Tempera paint
- Drawing paper
- Tinfoil plates

WHAT TO DO:

1. Onto the cardboard squares, glue the materials chosen with which to create the print; (in this example we chose macaroni)
2. Allow the glue to dry;
3. Dip the cardboard block into the paint;
4. Press block onto paper;
5. Repeat this action until desired effect is achieved;
6. Students may make a repeating or random pattern.

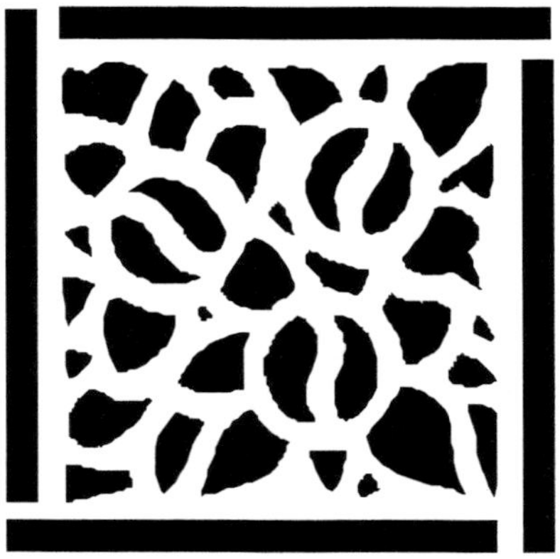

Print Making
Texture 2

Time Frame: 40 minutes

MOTIVATION:
Rubbing crayons or pastels over textured surfaces creates sample texture designs in this beginning lesson on texture and print making.

WHAT YOU NEED:
- Large sheets of newsprint
- Crayons or pastels
- Scissors

WHAT TO DO:
1. Fold the newsprint into 16 boxes;
2. Place one of the boxes over a textured surface;
3. Using the side of the crayon or pastel, rub the paper from edge to edge of the chosen box;
4. Repeat using different textures for each box until the paper is filled.

TEACHER TIP:
After the boxes have been filled, build an interesting picture by drawing on the back of the textured boxes. Cut out the picture and glue it to a piece of coloured construction paper, or manila paper and add details.

Basic Stenciling

Time Frame: 40 minutes

MOTIVATION:

After some exposure to stenciling, this technique can be used to create seasonal designs, as well as abstract shapes.

WHAT YOU NEED:

- Manila drawing paper
- Block paints
- Scissors
- Sponges
- Paper toweling
- Bristol board

WHAT TO DO:

1. Demonstrate for the students how to cut out an interesting shape in the centre of the Bristol board;
2. Pick up paint from the block paints using the sponge;
3. Pull the sponge from the edge of the "hole" in the Bristol board towards the center;
4. Cover the entire shape by streaking the paint towards the centre of the "hole";
5. Pat the stencil dry using the paper towel;
6. Move the stencil and repeat the process.

January Lessons

Try these art centres:

- ❖ Make an observational drawing of ice. Sketch fast!
- ❖ Try sculpting with tin foil. Twist and bend the foil into interesting shapes.
- ❖ Make a quick snowflake by folding and cutting white coffee filters!
- ❖ Draw a picture using white chalk on black paper.
- ❖ Practise filling in sections of a colouring page using tiny pieces shredded wool or yarn.
- ❖ Create a winter picture using cotton puffs, white wool, etc..

Print Making

Transfer Printing

Time Frame: 40 minutes

MOTIVATION:

Don't throw that old iron away! Use it instead as a tool in your art class.
Melting crayons are always fun. Watch as the heat creates new and wonderful prints!

WHAT YOU NEED:

- Iron
- Wax or finger painting paper
- Crayons
- Tissue paper

WHAT TO DO:

1. Demonstrate for the students how to draw an interesting picture on the glossy side of the finger painting paper or the wax paper;
2. Make sure there is a heavy layer of crayon on the paper and that the objects are clear and bright;
3. Place tissue paper over the drawing;
4. Using a hot iron, carefully press and lift iron. Do not slide iron over paper;
5. Peel tissue paper off wax paper or finger painting paper and reveal the transfer.

TEACHER TIP:

Try drawing on the rough side of sandpaper instead of the wax paper or finger painting paper. Use the iron to create "pointillism".

Mask Making

Time Frame: 40 minutes

MOTIVATION:

Masks play great importance in many cultures. Once masks are complete, the students may wish to perform in them. This technique involves creating firm felt forms for students to decorate.

WHAT YOU NEED:

- Piece of felt approximately 216 mm. X 279 mm. (8 ½" X 11")
- 250 ml. white glue
- Felt scraps, sequins, cotton balls, glitter, pipe cleaners, feathers, yarn, and other decorative materials
- Coffee can
- Plastic wrap
- Paint brush

WHAT TO DO:

1. Demonstrate for the students how to cut eye and mouth holes from the felt;
2. Cut the felt in a shape to cover the face, being mindful of the eye and mouth holes;
3. Cover the coffee can with plastic wrap;
4. Brush the glue over the felt, allowing the glue to soak into the felt;
5. Decorate the mask using the decorating materials collected;
6. Allow the mask to dry 24-48 hours;
7. Remove from coffee can;
8. Punch holes on either side for ribbon, string or wool to tie around head.

Cool Kaleidoscope

Time Frame: 40 minutes

MOTIVATION:

What could be more fun than watching your own kaleidoscope as bits and pieces of plastic form intricate shapes and designs?

WHAT YOU NEED:

- 2 film canisters, one clear and one black
- 3 small rectangular pieces of thin Plexiglas, about 2cm." X 6cm."
- Scissors
- Small piece of plastic wrap
- Black electrical tape
- Pieces of thin coloured plastic
- Nail and hammer

WHAT TO DO:

1. Demonstrate for the students how to use the electrical tape to tape the 3 (long sides) pieces of Plexiglas together to form a triangle;
2. Cover one end of the taped pieces of Plexiglas with plastic wrap, stretching it tightly;
3. Cut the pieces of thin colored plastic into tiny triangle or square shapes;
4. Place the pieces of colored plastic in the clear film canister;
5. Show the students how to push the Plexiglas shape with the plastic wrap first into the clear film canister;
6. Tell students not to push the Plexiglas shape all the way down into the clear container as the pieces should be able to move freely;
7. Using the nail and hammer, create a hole in the bottom of the black film canister;
8. Place the black canister over the other end of the Plexiglas shape;
9. Using the electrical tape the two film canisters together;
10. Point the clear canister towards the light and move the canisters to see the shapes fall and tumble, creating designs.

Cathay Edwards

Cathay Edwards is a Canadian artist born in Victoria British Columbia in 1961. She is the granddaughter of Marie Larivee, a Metis Native from Indian Head, Saskatchewan. Cathay still lives and paints in Victoria, and her paintings are vivid acrylic impressions of Vancouver Island landscapes and aboriginal carvings. See Cathay Edwards' art at: http://www.artistsincanada.com/php/homepage.php?id=6917

Time Frame: 40 minutes

MOTIVATION:

In this activity students will use mixed media to develop a painting in the style of Cathay Edwards. Students should be encouraged to look at the above website to see the art pieces: Burst, Spring Bunch, Lost Beneath the Watershed, or Summer Explosion for inspiration.

WHAT YOU NEED:

- Tempera paint
- Straws
- Brushes
- Markers
- Water
- Spoons
- Drawing paper

WHAT TO DO:

1. Demonstrate for the students how to create a background for their piece by dipping a spoon into the tempera paint and pouring it onto the drawing paper;
2. Show the students how to blow the paint across the paper creating shapes;
3. The students may wish to choose more than one colour and repeat the process;
4. Allow the piece to dry;
5. Once dry students outline the shapes using markers;
6. Add details to represent faces, plants, animals, etc. seen in the free form shapes.

February Art Lessons

Try these art centres:

- Paint a landscape using only shades of one colour.
- Stamp a picture using scrunched tin foil dipped in paint.
- Drop paint on top of white paper soaked with water.
- Practise colouring a colouring page using only different shades of pink and red.
- Hang a garland of lace and hearts around the classroom.
- Decorate the classroom door by gluing squares of white, red and pink construction paper on a paper panel the size of the door. Hang over door. Add hearts, cupids and flowers to the squares.

David Ruben Piqtoukun

Time Frame: 40 minutes

David Ruben Piqtoukun is an Inuit artist best known for his sculptures. He created an Inukshuk for the grounds of the McMichael Art Gallery. An Inukshuk is a landmark created from rock to resemble a human shape. They stand out on the flat landscape of the Arctic. They can indicate directional markers, religious icons, or hunting grounds. Inukshuks still stand in many areas of the Arctic, some dating before 1000 B.C.. You may visit David Ruben Piqtoukun's Inukshuk at: **http://www.mcmichael.com/sculpture-piqtoukun.shtml**

Inukshuks

MOTIVATION:

This is a great activity for students to try after becoming acquainted with the shapes and reasons for Inukshuks

WHAT YOU NEED:

- Large piece of light blue construction paper
- Construction paper in various colours
- Glue

WHAT TO DO:

1. Use the large sheet of light blue construction paper as the background for this activity;
2. Demonstrate for the students how to use the thumb and forefinger to tear the construction paper shapes;
3. Begin by tearing grey or brown construction paper into shapes that resemble large stones;
4. Show the students how to arrange the shapes into a human form;
5. Glue the shape onto the light blue construction paper;
6. Tearing items from the other coloured construction paper, create a scene for the Inukshuk. (Details may include Inuit hunters, houses, fishing, polar bears, etc.)

Reflection in a Pond

Time Frame: 40 minutes

MOTIVATION:
This drawing uses mixed media to produce a lovely scenic picture.

WHAT YOU NEED:

- Oil pastels
- Manila paper
- Paint wash in dark colour
- Spoon or similar item to use to rub
- Paintbrush

WHAT TO DO:

1. Demonstrate for the children how to fold their manila paper lengthwise;
2. Above the fold draw a meadow using heavy application of the oil pastel;
3. Add details to the picture such as trees, grass, barn, cows, clouds in the sky, etc. to create a pastoral scene;
4. Fold the top half of the paper onto the bottom half;
5. Using the spoon or other such item, rub the surface of the paper to transfer the drawing to the bottom half;
6. Open the paper;
7. Paint over the top half of the scene with the colour wash;
8. Add water to the wash and paint over the bottom half of the paper to create a lighter effect;
9. Over the water, brush some streaks of green, white and blue paint to create ripples;
10. When dry, using a yellow oil pastel, add a moon, stars and lights to any buildings;
11. Re-fold the painting and rub again with the spoon to transfer the details of the night effects.

Patterns and Cuts

Time Frame: 40 minutes

MOTIVATION:

Collage is a technique of gluing shapes onto a sheet to create a picture. By moving paint over the paper using different materials, or items, texture is created. This activity combines these two techniques making an effective scene.

WHAT YOU NEED:

- Thick paint in a variety of colours
- Items to create patterns in the paint (cardboard with notches cut into it, pencils with the lead broken, fork, fingers, etc.)
- Scissors
- Glue
- White paper in two sizes, 81/2" X 11" and 12"X14

WHAT TO DO:

1. Using several pieces of 81/2"X11"paper, create a texture on each piece;
2. Allow each piece to dry;
3. On the larger piece of paper, design a scene, such as an underwater picture;
4. Using the dried textured papers, cut a background, middle ground and foreground;
5. Glue onto the 12"X14" design;
6. Add details by cutting items such as fish, coral, kelp, etc. from the remaining textured papers;
7. Voila! Collage and texture technique.

Paper Clay "Planetscape"

Time Frame: 40 minutes

MOTIVATION:

Craters, valleys, flat mountains and swirling gases are familiar words to describe the surfaces of unknown planets. In this activity, challenge your students to create a new planet surface.

MATERIALS:

- An old blender (optional)
- Paper mache egg cartons or coffee trays
- White glue
- Paint, (sparkles, glitter, etc. optional)
- Brushes
- Water
- Newspaper
- Wax paper

WHAT TO DO:

1. Prepare the clay by tearing the egg cartons or coffee trays into bits and soaking them in water overnight;
2. Begin by brainstorming words with the students that describe planet surfaces;
3. Explain to the students that they will be able to create their own "planetscape" in this activity;
4. Drain the egg carton material and pulverize it in the blender or by squeezing your through fingers;
5. Add enough white glue until material is the consistency of clay;
6. Give each student a quantity of "clay" on a pad of newspaper which has a piece of wax paper covering it;
7. Allow the student to create a "planetscape";
8. Paint and add details such as sparkles, aliens etc.

March Art Lessons

Try these art centres:

- ❖ Draw faces, bodies and heads overlapping to look like a crowd of people.
- ❖ Begin to draw a picture. After two minutes pass it along to a neighbour. Keep changing and adding until everyone has contributed to each other's picture!
- ❖ Colour a colouring picture using pencil crayons and only short curly strokes. For example: cccc
- ❖ Use fluorescent paint blown through a straw onto black construction paper to create creatures. Use markers to add details.

Watercolour Techniques

Time Frame: 40 minutes

Motivation:

Exploring the medium of watercolour is an excellent way for students to understand the basic techniques used in generating watercolour paintings. Watercolours make wonderful and unusual creations when paint is "floated " on watercolour paper. It becomes obvious after painting that control and understanding of the medium is necessary to produce good results. Students will experiment with techniques such as wet-on-wet, dry-on-dry and wet-on-dry, etc.

What you need:

- Watercolour paper (small 8cm X 12cm)
- Brushes
- Paper towels
- Styrofoam plates
- Watercolour paints (those plastic boxes of paint found in most children's art supplies are watercolour paints!)
- Water (two containers)

What to do:

1. Allow the children to feel the difference in the watercolour paper;
2. Explain that the watercolour paper is specially formulated to withstand wetness, allowing watercolours to float on the surface of the paper for longer periods of time;
3. List on a piece of chart paper or blackboard the various techniques to be used, such as wet-on-wet, dry-on-dry and wet-on-dry;
4. Remind the children to write on the back of each piece of paper the technique they intend to try. For example the teacher will start with wet-on-wet and write that on the back of the paper;
5. Explain to the students, a wash is a very thin coat of paint, and you can see the paper beneath a wash because it is transparent;
6. Tell the students that washes are created using a technique called "wet-on-wet." (This means they are painting with a wet brush on wet paper);
7. Demonstrate for the students how to take a thick brush and paint clean water evenly across the paper; (note that the paper should become wet, but not drippy and there should be no puddles);
8. Select a colour and paint across the paper in a horizontal band;
9. Continue with the same colour or choose another and paint a band next to it. Explain that you brush once or twice, but don't go back and brush over it. The paint should blend;
10. Allow the paper to dry.

Teacher Tip:

Dry-on-dry means to blot your brush dry and apply it to dry paper. Wet-on-dry means you work with a wet brush on dry paper. Painting wet-on-dry is best suited for painting areas that need greater control and more intense colours. Encourage students to paint abstract shapes and lines, and to experiment with the brush as well as the amount of paint and water used. Blend colors noting how they bleed when they hit other wet spots and stay put when they are applied to dry paper.

Salt Prints

Time Frame: 40 minutes

MOTIVATION:
By sprinkling salt over wet paint, beautiful creations can be made. The salt alters the paint creating a splotched cloud-like effect.

WHAT YOU NEED:

- Water colour paint
- Brushes
- Water
- Sea salt (will work with table salt, but the effect will not be as good)
- Drawing paper

WHAT TO DO:

1. Demonstrate for the students how to float large areas of colour onto the drawing paper. Float by loading your brush with lots of paint;
2. While the paint is still wet, sprinkle salt over the surface of the paint;
3. Allow the salt print to dry;
4. Brush salt off paper.

TEACHER TIP:
Use this technique as part of a larger scene, such as a seascape, outer space scene, etc.
After the painting is dry, cut sections out to use as part of a collage.

Maud Lewis

Maud Dowley Lewis was born in 1903, in South Ohio, Nova Scotia. Maud and her mother painted Christmas cards to sell to friends and neighbours. In 1938 Maud Dowley wed Everett Lewis and lived with him in a tiny house where there was no indoor plumbing, radio, television or electricity! She posted a sign on the roadside by her house, announcing her art for sale. Newspaper and magazine articles, as well as television documentaries made Maud a well known folk artist. Orders for paintings came from far and wide. Maud died in 1970.

Time Frame: 40 minutes

MOTIVATION:

Folk Artists are typically from rural regions, and are more closely related to craftsmen than fine artists. The folk art style is characterized by a lack of traditional rules of perspective and proportion. Other names for folk art are tole painting, self-taught art, or primitive art.

WHAT YOU NEED:

- Tempera or acrylic paint
- Brushes
- Manila paper

WHAT TO DO:

1. Discuss with the children the possible scenes for their piece;
2. Point out to the students the simplicity and "flat" feeling that gives folk art its characteristics;
3. Demonstrate for the children how to paint a background;
4. Allow the paint to dry between applications;
5. Add details to finish the painting.

Harry's Castle Creations

Time Frame: 40 minutes

MOTIVATION:

This activity is good to do after a discussion on the middle ages, Halloween haunted castles or after reading novels about castles and wizards!

WHAT YOU NEED:

- Paper roll tubes
- Bristol board
- Glue
- Paint
- Brushes
- Water
- Toothpicks
- Newspaper
- Popsicle sticks

WHAT TO DO:

1. Demonstrate for the students how to cut the tops of the paper rolls to resemble the tops of castle turrets;
2. Create four walls of the castle by cutting the Bristol board into 4 equal pieces;
3. Cut the edges of the Bristol board to make battlements or gaps along the tops;
4. Using the paper roll tubes as corners, glue the four pieces of Bristol board to form the walls of the castle;
5. Paint the castle shades of grey;
6. While the structure dries, create a draw bridge by gluing the Popsicle sticks together;
7. Glue the toothpicks together to form a grid to act as a gate or portcullis, which can be placed over the opening of the draw bridge;
8. Cut a semi-circular opening on the front of the castle to create a door;
9. Attach the drawbridge "open" at the mouth of the door;
10. Attach the toothpick gate over the opening;
11. Using markers, add details to the castle, such as windows or bricks.

Modern-Day Pointillism

Time Frame: 40 minutes

MOTIVATION:

Impressionist painters used small dots of paint to create pictures. In this activity, students can create the impressionist technique using markers or crayons.

WHAT YOU NEED:

- Markers or crayons
- Manila paper
- Tempera paint, which has been diluted with water
- Brushes
- Pencil

WHAT TO DO:

1. Before beginning the activity, discuss impressionism with the students; (Georges Seurat is a good example to use.)
2. Demonstrate for the students how to lightly sketch a picture using the pencil on the manila paper;
3. Using the diluted tempera paint, wash over the large areas of the picture;
4. Once dry, use the markers or crayons to turn this into an impressionists painting by "dotting" in details!

April Art Lessons

Try these art centres:

- ❖ Draw a dove using a black marker. Add lines radiating from the dove and colour the areas created in different colours.
- ❖ Draw an observational drawing of a person's eye, hand or ear.
- ❖ Tear mountain shapes from black construction paper and add details the landscape
- ❖ Tear construction paper shapes. Colour along the torn edge, lay it on black paper and rub down with paper towels to transfer the chalk to the black paper.

Easter and Earth Day Activities

Puffy Eggs

Have children cut oval shapes from construction paper. On the oval shape using water-based markers, instruct children to create interesting line patterns (e.g., jagged, wavy, thick and thin.) Trace over the water based marker with white glue to produce a puffy effect.

Eggs To Dye For!

Have children carefully draw designs on hard-boiled eggs using a crayon. Dip the hard-boiled eggs into dye baths created with food colouring, water and a bit of vinegar. As an alternative to food colouring, use jelly powders or crystal drink mixes diluted with water.

Earth Day Bird Feeders

Collect pinecones. Coat pinecones with peanut butter or suet. Roll the coated pinecones in birdseed and hang in a nearby tree. Watch for the feasting birds.

Earth Day Collage

Have children create collages using magazine pictures of animals and natural resources such as water. Once the whole paper is covered, encourage children to find and cut out words or phrases to promote Earth Day awareness. For example, “Stop Pollution” or “The Earth is for everybody”.

El Greco (1541-1614)

Domenikos Theotokopoulos was his real name, but when El Greco moved to Spain in 1577, people began to call him El Greco, "the Greek". El Greco is known for long tall figures in his paintings. The people seemed to be stretched out with thin arms, legs, necks and faces. He was the first of the great artists to believe art should show feelings, and he often used the colour blue to express emotion.

Time Frame: 40 minutes

MOTIVATION:

Try stretching out a picture to create thin people, or as a variation, wide people.

WHAT YOU NEED:

- Pictures of people cut from magazines
- Scissors
- Glue
- Pencils
- Erasers
- Tracing or similar paper
- Ruler
- Manila paper
- Scrap paper
- Colouring materials or painting materials

WHAT TO DO:

1. Demonstrate for the children how to choose a picture from a magazine of a person's head or body;
2. Using a pencil and ruler, draw strips across the picture, dividing it into equal pieces;
3. Show the children how to carefully cut the picture apart;
4. Using the scrap paper, reassemble the picture, leaving about 2-3 centimetres between each piece;
5. Place a sheet of tracing paper, or other paper you can see through over top of the glued sections;
6. Trace around the glued down picture creating a new version of a "stretched out "person;
7. Demonstrate for the children how to rub the side of the pencil over the back of the tracing paper, to create "carbon" paper;
8. Lay the tracing paper face down on a fresh sheet of manila paper;
9. With a dull pencil, go over the "stretched out person" transferring the new picture to the manila paper;
10. Complete the new picture by colouring or painting.

Shadow Butterflies

Time Frame: 40 minutes

MOTIVATION:

These three dimensional butterflies create a spring festival in the classroom.

WHAT YOU NEED:

- Construction paper, both light and dark colours
- Scissors
- Pipe cleaners
- Glue
- Pencil

WHAT TO DO:

1. Fold one piece of light coloured construction paper in half;
2. Draw a butterfly shape along the fold of the paper;
3. Cut the butterfly out;
4. Keeping the butterfly folded, cut sections from the wings; (similar to cutting out a snowflake pattern)
5. Fold a darker colour of construction paper, (this will create the shadow);
6. Place the folded light coloured butterfly on top of the dark construction paper, matching folds and trace around the light butterfly;
7. Remove the light butterfly and add about 2 centimetres around the edge of the trace line on the dark coloured butterfly;
8. Cut the dark coloured paper butterfly out;
9. Bend one pipe cleaner in half;
10. Attach pipe cleaners to the head of the dark coloured butterfly;
11. Place cut out butterfly on top of the dark coloured butterfly and glue along the body section.
12. Hang butterfly with a shadow to display

Print Making

Mono-printing with Paint

Time Frame: 40 minutes

MOTIVATION:

Taking a print from a painted picture can create interesting and imaginative prints.

WHAT YOU NEED:

- Vinyl or plastic placemats (solid colours are best)
- Detergent
- Paint
- Brushes
- Newsprint
- Sponge or paper towels
- Water

WHAT TO DO:

1. Add a few drops of detergent to the paint. This will keep it from beading up on the vinyl;
2. Using the paint and detergent mixture, quickly paint a picture on the vinyl placemat; (Waiting will allow the paint to dry and there will not be a good print)
3. Cover the placemat with a sheet of newsprint;
4. Rub over the entire surface of the newsprint from the center to the edges;
5. Carefully peel the newsprint off the placemat;
6. Clean placemat with water and sponge or paper towel.

Hoñgeeýesa

Hoñgeeýesa was an Assiniboine Native. His artwork was discovered on the back of ledger paper. Often Natives used the backs of the accountant's papers for sketches and drawings. In 1996, the Glenbow Museum toured Canada with an exhibition showing drawings by an unknown Native artist. Members of Carry The Kettle First Nations and the Touchwood-File Hills Qu'Appelle Tribal Council were able to collaborate with the Glenbow's exhibition curator and accredit the drawings to Hoñgeeýesa.

Time Frame: 40 minutes

MOTIVATION:

Ledger drawings were often done on lined Indian Agent or accountant's paper. Visit http://www.glenbow.org/arthtm/ledger.htm to see examples of Hoñgeeýesa's work.

WHAT YOU NEED:

- Brown paper bags
- Watercolour paint
- Brushes
- Pencils
- Sponge
- Water

WHAT TO DO:

1. Demonstrate for the students how to wipe the brown paper bag with a wet sponge to soften paper;
2. Show the students how to gently crumple the shopping bag into a large ball, to further soften the paper;
3. After the paper has dried, have the students sketch a story using only pictographs and symbols;
4. Using watercolour paints, fill in the pencil sketches.

Shadow Dancing

Time Frame: 40 minutes

Motivation:

In this activity, students will create shadows that attach to their drawings of an action figure!

What you need:

- White drawing paper
- Black construction paper
- Larger sheet of contrasting coloured construction paper
- Glue
- Scissors
- Stapler

What to do:

1. Demonstrate for the children how to sketch an action figure, such as a runner or basketball player onto the white paper;
2. Place the black and the white paper together, stapling in the corners to keep the papers from slipping;
3. Carefully cut out the figure that was drawn on the white paper;
4. Fold the larger sheet of contrasting construction paper in half;
5. Lay the white figure on the upper half of the paper;
6. Lay the "shadow" on the lower half of the paper;
7. Add details to the white figure.

May Art Lessons

Try these art centres:

- Colour a colouring page by pasting tiny pieces of magazines to create an interesting effect. Keep containers handy of different colours from magazines.
- Tear mountain shapes from manila paper and glue to black construction paper and add details to the landscape
- With a partner, draw curved, zig-zaged and spiral lines around the paper. Turn the paper until you see a shape or an idea that can be used. Fill in the details.
- Do a blind contour drawing of feet, hands, or an object in the classroom.

Paper Mask Making

Time Frame: 40 minutes

MOTIVATION:

After a discussion of the importance of masks in many cultures, students can make their own. This technique involves manipulating and layering paper into curls and folds to create a three-dimensional effect.

WHAT YOU NEED:

- Construction paper in a variety of colours and sizes
- Glue
- Hole punch
- Scissors
- Decorating materials (the left-over holes from a three-hole punch, etc.)

WHAT TO DO:

1. Demonstrate for the children a variety of paper sculpting techniques such as curling the paper by passing it gently over the blades of scissors, for hair – folding a triangular piece for noses - curving for eyelids - crimping for hair – etc;
2. Demonstrate how to fold the paper in half;
3. Draw a contour for a mask, making a semi-circle;
4. Cut out the semi-circle;
5. Hold the paper vertically, cut a small slit in the center top and bottom;
6. Demonstrate how to glue the slits across each other to make a three-dimensional form;
7. Remind the students of the symmetry of a face;
8. Build features on the three-dimensional form;
9. Students should consider adding horns, hair, beards, etc.

Optical Illusions

Time Frame: 40 minutes

MOTIVATION:

The use of geometric shapes is common in optical illusion. Working to create an optical illusion will give students experience with positive and negative shape, as well as contrast and pattern.

WHAT YOU NEED:

- Drawing paper
- Rulers, circle templates (plastic lids work well)
- Markers
- Pencils
- Erasers

WHAT TO DO:

1. Demonstrate for the students how to trace the width of the ruler along the paper, creating vertical lines, by lining up the ruler vertically along the short edge of the paper;
2. Draw at least 5 different geometric shapes of different sizes on the paper in an interesting design; (Shapes could include squares, diamonds, stars, rectangles, octagons, triangles, etc.)
3. Using the markers colour the first column, but omit the space inside the geometric shape; (plan ahead of time which sections will be coloured, by placing a light X on the section)
4. In the second column, colour all the inside the spaces of the geometric shape; (the opposite of the first column.)
5. The third column omit the space inside the geometric shape; (opposite of the second column, same as the first)
6. Continue across the paper, one column at a time, alternating coloured with white shapes and white with coloured shapes.
7. When all the columns are finished, colour all the white shapes with a contrasting coloured marker to complete the optical illusion.

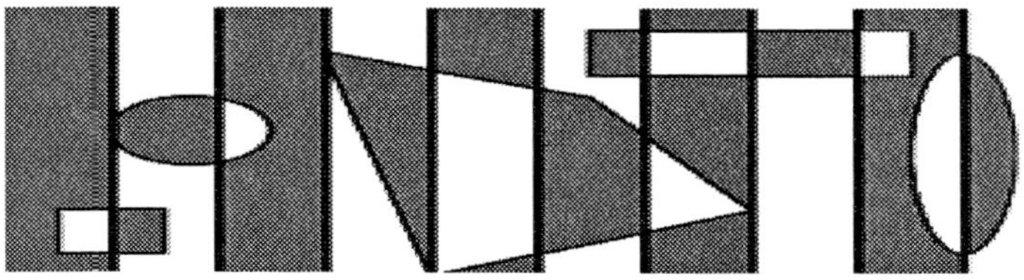

Fred Brown

Fred Brown lives in British Columbia, Canada. He is a print artist who is becoming more and more internationally renown. Much of his inspiration comes from nature, and many of his prints are made from woodcarvings. His techniques, process and works of art may be discovered at: http://www.fredbrowntheartist.com/process.htm

---

Print Making With Styrofoam Plates

Time Frame: 40 minutes

MOTIVATION:

Printing from Styrofoam plates is a technique in which the results are similar to printing from woodcarvings. The students should be made aware of the positive and negative spaces created by removing or compressing the foam plate.

WHAT YOU NEED:

- Styrofoam plates
- Pencils (preferable ones that are dull)
- Manila paper
- Tempera paint
- Brushes

WHAT TO DO:

1. Demonstrate for the student how to gently press the pencil into the Styrofoam plate making indentations;
2. Discuss with the students the positive and negative spaces created by the carving of the Styrofoam plate;
3. Have the students create a pencil drawing the same size as the Styrofoam plate;
4. Using a dull pencil show the students how to transfer the drawing to the bottom of the Styrofoam plate;
5. Brush the tempera paint over the bottom of the Styrofoam plate;
6. Carefully press the plate down onto the manila paper;
7. Peel the Styrofoam plate off the manila paper revealing the print.

June Art Lessons

Try these art centres:

- ❖ Draw a large rectangle on paper. Place twenty black dots anywhere on the paper. Beginning at one end of the paper, draw horizontal lines, making a bulge over each dot. Colour and see the tunnel effect!

- ❖ Trace your hand, then draw 8 lines anywhere on the paper including through the hand. Colour the sections. Try not to put two colours beside each other.

- ❖ Follow the contour lines of your name. Make each line a different colour.

- ❖ Make three grab bags with nouns, adjectives and verbs. Select a word from each bag and paint your sentence. (cold dog driving)

Mosaic

The Mayan and Aztec natives of Mexico made mosaics from semi-precious stones. The mosaics decorated masks, shields, and helmets. In Roman times, mosaics decorated floors, fountains and baths.

Time Frame: 40 minutes

Motivation:

In this activity students will use grains, beans and various found materials to create mosaic pictures.

What you need:

- Beans –lima, white, red, kidney, mung, etc.
- Lentils
- Pebbles (if you have unlimited budget, aquarium gravel is effective!)
- Sand
- Glue
- Pencils
- Bristol board

What to do:

1. Demonstrate for the students how to draw a picture in pencil, on the Bristol board;
2. Glue the various materials onto the design;
3. Frame or mount the piece.

Tom Thomson

Tom Thomson was born near Claremont, Ontario and inspired a group of Canadian artist known as the "Group of Seven". He drowned in Canoe Lake in 1917, just three years before the Group of Seven held their first exhibition. He drew many scenes from Algonquin Park in Ontario. The group of artists showed foreground, middle ground, and background, by painting what seemed to be "layers". They tied the painting together by joining the bottom to the top by making things, like trees, reaching across the painting. View more examples of painting by Tom Thomson and the Group of Seven on the Internet site: www.mcmichael.com

---

Time Frame: 40 minutes

MOTIVATION:

Students will to try to create the same effect that the group of seven did using layers of paint and construction paper.

WHAT YOU NEED:

- Construction paper
- Glue
- Scissors
- Pencil

WHAT TO DO:

1. Demonstrate for children how to sketch a picture including a background, middle ground and foreground. You may wish to try making the mountains as a background, a lake or river as the middle ground and a forest or cabin as the foreground;
2. Fill in the sketch with blocks of colour;
3. Cut construction paper to the shapes of the mountains, lakes and trees to add depth and detail;
4. Remember to attach the drawing together by planning a tree or rock formation that flows from the bottom of the picture to the top to tie it together;
5. Glue the shapes down to make a landscape picture, just like the Group of Seven.

Ruins of Clay

Time Frame: 40 minutes

MOTIVATION:

The Greek Ruins and temples show us ancient stones and weathered structures. They make an excellent reference for this project.

WHAT YOU NEED:

- Sand
- Glue
- Plastiscene
- Scissors
- Cardboard (box lid is best)

WHAT TO DO:

1. Demonstrate for the students how to form the cardboard into a raised platform, if a box lid is not available; (optional, the teacher may wish to leave the cardboard flat and use it as a base)
2. Spread a thin coat of glue over the cardboard and cover with sand; (Shake off excess sand into a container to prevent messy floors!)
3. Mould the plastiscene into columns and arches;
4. Using the scissors, score textures and cracks, etc. into the columns and arches;
5. Place a finger into the sand and press it onto the plastiscene columns and arches, allowing the traces of sand to be embedded into the plastiscene;
6. Arrange the columns and arches on the cardboard base or box lid;
7. Add clay pots, stones, and scrolls to the scene!

Pitseolak Ashoona

Pitseeolak Ashoona was born in 1904, on Nottingham Island. She moved with her family along the coastal areas of Cape Dorset. As an artist Pitseolak worked hard to produce sculptures and prints that made people think about Inuit art. In the twenty years she worked as an artist, she made over 7,000 drawings and 250 prints. She was awarded the Order of Canada in 1977, a very special award that is given to people who make an important contribution to Canada. Pitseolak Ashoona died in 1983.

"Sand" Sculpture

Time Frame: 40 minutes

MOTIVATION:

Follow the recipe to make a great sand medium for sculpting. Mix ahead so students can be ready to experiment when the lesson is taught.

Make sand clay by combining 250 ml. of cornstarch, 500ml. of sifted sand and 325ml. of water. Cook the mixture in an old pot for 10 minutes, or until the mixture leaves the side of the pot. Cool, knead and store in an airtight container.

WHAT YOU NEED:

- One recipe of sand clay
- Carving "tools" such as plastic utensils
- Newspaper

WHAT TO DO:

1. Demonstrate for the students how to mould the sand clay into a shape suitable for carving;
2. Using the plastic forks, knives and spoons, add details to carve an animal or Inuit form.

Brain Gone to Mush?

TEACHER TIP: Sometimes trying to think of an idea to stimulate creative painting or drawing can be difficult. Try these ideas:

1. Paint a beach ball rolling across the sand.
2. Paint a boat on a lake on a sunny day.
3. Paint a bowl of fruit.
4. Paint a plane in the sky.
5. Paint a watering can in a garden.
6. Paint a child flying a kite.
7. Paint a bird in a tree.
8. Paint a skier on a snow hill.
9. Paint a water skier on a lake.
10. Paint a close up of a flower.
11. Paint a self-portrait.
12. List 10 things a colour reminds you of.
13. Draw something you fear.
14. Draw yourself angry, sad, afraid, etc.
15. Draw something that opens and closes.
16. Draw a creature that hatches.
17. Draw your happiest moment.
18. Create a picture using only line, shape, colour, etc.
19. Use a postcard as inspiration.
20. Paint your favourite food item.

Great Websites to Explore

http://www.artsconnected.org/toolkit/explore.cfm
This site has all the elements listed, where students can investigate the principles of line, design, composition etc. through an interactive toolkit.

http://www.eduweb.com/insideart/
A really neat experience where student become part of a story created through paintings.

http://www.eduweb.com/pintura/index.html
This online game is about art history and art composition. In the game, you play a 1940's noir detective with a degree in art history. Students can play the game independently or in small groups.

http://www.moma.org/index.html
This is the Museum of Modern Art site in New York City. Students can view collections of famous artists.

http://www.civilisations.ca/aborig/haida/haaindxe.html
Students can explore the art and the culture of the Haida Nation.

http://www.artcyclopedia.com/
This site has it all. Looking for an artist, an artistic movement, medium, women as artists? This is where you can start your search. Compare Munch's Starry Night with Van Gogh's Starry Night using this site!

http://cybermuse.gallery.ca/cybermuse/teachers/index_e.jsp
This site is designed to help teachers integrate art into their curriculum. There are on line resources for exploration of themes, collections class activities and lesson plans.

http://www.wildlifeart.org/Rungius/index.html
Learn how to use art principles like balance, contrast, movement, and proportion to compose a work of art. Create a composition with a famous wildlife artist.

http://www.virtualmuseum.ca/Exhibitions/Gestes/anglais/index.html
An exhibition of French Canadian culture and art across Canada.

http://www.emilycarr.ca/
A great website that displays almost all of Carr's works, as well as a great teacher's guide.

http://www.glenbow.org/art.htm
This site focuses on artwork in the Canadian Northwest, including Inuit and Native artwork.

http://www.tomthomson.org/groupseven/index.html
Visit the Group of Seven through the Tom Thompson website.

http://www.drawnonward.com/
An interesting site of contemporary Canadian artists who quite possibly could be the new group of seven!

Assessment and Evaluation

Artist Portfolio and Journal

An artist portfolio with a journal, is an excellent way for children to organize their thoughts and ideas about the art concepts presented. Grammar, spelling, or syntax in the journal entry should not be emphasized. The student responses give the teacher opportunities to plan follow up activities that may review and clarify concepts learned. In addition, a portfolio is a wonderful keepsake to show off a student's artistic abilities.

Art journal entries may be done intermittently depending on scheduling. Entries should be brief. Time allotted for completion should be less than fifteen minutes. Entries can be done with a whole group, small group or an individual.

Art Journal Entries can include:

- Direct instructions by the teacher;
- Key ideas;
- Personal reflections;
- Questions that arise;
- Connections discovered;
- Problem solving strategies.

Assessment Journal

Thinking About My Art

In my artwork, I did a good job on:

____

Next time I would like to:

____

My Artwork Plan

Name of art project: ______________________________

I am going to use the following art materials:

Crayons _____ Pencil crayons ____ Paint_____

Construction Paper____ White Paper _____ Other _____

Thinking About Art

Name of art project

____

This piece of art makes me think about:

____